A Journey to Redemption

Finding Hope, Grace, and Restoration in God's Unfailing Love

Tony Mejia

ISBN: 979-8-8690-8626-6

ACKNOWLEDGMENTS

I would like to express my heartfelt gratitude to my wife for her unwavering support throughout the entire process of writing this second book. She has been an immense help and has played a crucial role in my personal growth. I also want to thank my children for always believing in me. Life hasn't been easy, but I have learned the importance of surrounding myself with people who encourage progress and help me reach my goals. In times when life throws curveballs, having the right support system makes all the difference. I am especially grateful for placing God at the center of everything. I extend my thanks to my pastors for being there for us and for their unwavering belief in us as we walk on God's path. I hope and pray that those who relate to my story understand that it is never too late to rise and let God take control. Lastly, I want to express my deep appreciation to my parents, Julio Mejia and Zelandia Mauricio, for being with me through all the hardships, ups, and downs. They are a significant part of my testimony, and I will always cherish and love them.

To protect privacy, the names of all individuals mentioned in my testimony have been changed to avoid any form of recognition.

CONTENTS

TONY MEJIA
A JOURNEY
to Repentance
Finding Hope, Grace, and Restoration
in God's Unfailing Love

Prologue

When reading this book written by my husband, Tony Mejía, in each chapter you will find a lived testimony. From the depths of his heart, he wanted to share with each one of you very personal experiences that marked his life in one way or another. Tony shares different experiences or stages of his life away from God and the process of reconciliation. In his journey of having drifted away from God at one point in his life, he experienced fear, hopelessness, discouragement, doubt, among other things, reaching a point where he grew tired of living an empty life and decided to surrender his heart to God once again. Since that moment, God has brought joy, peace, happiness, and, above all, the promise of eternal life into his life. Living for God is a calling to live a life full of love, compassion, and acceptance for others. I know many will be able to identify themselves when reading this powerful testimony. Tony wants us to know that no matter how many times you fall, you can always get back up. God awaits you with open arms to restore you.

Heidy Mejía

New Life in Christ

My life has undergone a remarkable transformation for the better. Since deepening my relationship with God, I have experienced a profound sense of fulfillment. Everything in Florida seems different now that I have surrendered my life to Christ. I have left behind my former habits of drinking, drug use, and selfish living, and now strive to live according to God's will. My greatest desire is to be in God's presence, and as I reflect on my journey, I am reminded of my grandmother's wise teachings. She would often speak to me about the importance of fasting, praying, reading God's word, and humbling oneself before Him. These practices have helped me to stay connected to God and to embrace a spiritual way of life. I truly feel like a brand-new person.

One passage that resonates with me is 2 Corinthians 5:16–17, which states, "So if anyone is in Christ, he is a new creation: everything old has passed away; see, everything has become new!" Sometimes, this verse may be incorrectly understood as focusing solely on individual believers being made new in Christ. However, it is important to also consider Romans 12:2, where we are reminded not to conform to the patterns of this world, but to be transformed by the renewing of our minds. Through this transformation, we can discern God's will and live in a manner that is good, acceptable, and perfect.

Another impactful passage is found in John 3:1-8, where Jesus engages in a conversation with Nicodemus. In this discussion, Jesus emphasizes the need for spiritual rebirth to enter the kingdom of God. Jesus explains that being born again involves being born of both water and the Spirit. Just as something born of the flesh is fleshly, something born of the Spirit is spiritual. This passage reinforces the notion of transformation and being born anew in Christ.

These verses emphasize the call for us to undergo a transformative journey. Our old selves have passed away, and we are called to embrace our new identities in

Christ. No longer can we offer excuses or continue living as we once did. Personally, I have witnessed a stark contrast between my former life and the life I now lead in Christ. While I used to be driven by carnal desires, I am now compelled by the promptings of the Holy Spirit. Drawing closer to God has been an amazing experience, and the intimacy I have developed with Him is something that no one can take away from me.

At the start of my walk with Christ, I could clearly hear His voice. Although it may have seemed strange to others, I knew without a doubt that I was communing with God and that He was listening to me. However, as I embarked on this new spiritual journey, I also encountered challenges. I found myself in spiritual battles, learning to navigate a whole new way of living. In my apartment, I experienced unsettling encounters with what seemed to be demonic forces. Every time I fell asleep, I would awaken with the sensation of someone ominously watching over me. I would hastily turn on the light, breathing heavily, only to find that no one was there. This fear escalated to the point where I felt compelled to sleep with the light on.

As I continue this path, I am reminded that spiritual growth often comes with moments of adversity. However, I firmly believe that God's presence in my life has given me the strength to overcome these challenges. I am grateful for the transformation that has taken place and for the new life I have found in Christ.

I vividly recall the discipline and guidance provided by my fellow brother in Christ who devoted his time to teaching me about walking with God. He consistently prayed for me and reminded me that the enemy was distressed at losing one soul. Previously, the Bible seemed inscrutable to me, but inexplicably, I began to comprehend its teachings. As my spiritual battle intensified and daunting challenges materialized, an unprecedented sense of peace enveloped me. I resolved to protect this newfound peace at all costs, heeding my grandmother's advice to engage in fasting and fervent prayer.

One day, I sat down to watch "The Passion of Christ," yearning to witness firsthand the magnitude of Jesus' sacrifice for humanity. Gripped by overwhelming emotion, tears streamed down my face as I expressed profound gratitude for Jesus' salvation and forgiveness of my sins. Suddenly, during the scene depicting Jesus' impending sacrifice, an ominous sound emanated from my door, as though someone were attempting to force their way inside. Startled, I leapt to my feet and flung the door open, only to find no one there. Disturbed by this unsettling occurrence, I immediately contacted the brother from my church, recounting the incident to him. Alarmed, he advised, "I must come to your house and anoint it; the enemy is attempting to instill fear within you."

Upon his arrival, the brother initiated a powerful prayer session, stressing the necessity of purging my dwelling of any remnants of my past life. Committed to my transformation, I discarded all traces of drugs. This experience was nothing short of extraordinary. Prior to embracing Christ, I remained oblivious to the existence of the spiritual realm, but now, through my faith, its reality became irrefutable.

In Florida, a deep sense of loneliness permeated my days, prompting a divine prompting for a fresh start in my hometown of Lawrence. Consequently, I returned home, where I found solace living with my parents. Initially skeptical of my profound transformation, my parents slowly witnessed the tangible impact it had on my countenance—I radiated an inner glow. My life veered onto a new course, as my primary focus became prayer, sleeping on the floor, fasting, and immersing myself in the Word of God. Remarkable spiritual encounters became commonplace. Though perplexed by my unwavering devotion, my parents, along with my sister Nana, began accompanying me to church, fostering an atmosphere of collective worship. We all embraced the same gospel-centered music, listened to sermons, and engaged in family Bible studies that mirrored miniature services held within our home.

A Journey of Redemption

During her visits from the Dominican Republic, my beloved grandmother, affectionately called Mama Luz, derived immeasurable joy from witnessing our family's transformation—from division and indulgence to unity in Christ. Her prayers and scriptural wisdom provided unwavering support, culminating in a breakthrough after her forty-day fast. She rejoiced in the Lord, for she had sought His intervention in our family for more than two decades. To all the women, men, and young individuals reading this book, I offer an earnest piece of advice: continue praying and placing your trust in God, for He is at work. Even during moments when it seems unlikely that God will answer your prayers, remain steadfast, for His timing is impeccable. This is precisely what my grandmother exemplified, ultimately witnessing divine favor unfurl in her life.

During this period, I found myself attending two different churches where I met many inspiring young individuals who were on fire for God. I eagerly participated in various events and gatherings, yet I soon realized it was time to choose a single church to call home. Eventually, I made the decision to join Ebenezer, and I began attending baptism classes, a pivotal moment in transforming my life. Though I still held onto my old attire and earrings, there was an undeniable fire burning within me.

It was during a special service with a renowned

preacher that I had a profound revelation. That night, I understood that God wanted me to make significant changes in every aspect of my life. Suddenly, I no longer felt a desire to wear my earrings or dress in a way that reflected a more urban lifestyle. God worked swiftly and visibly in my life, and His favor was evident to all who observed me. Being part of a Spanish-speaking church also allowed me to improve my command of my native language, which had faded over time due to my upbringing in the United States.

It was imperative for me to address some lingering doubts regarding my two children, both of whom I had fathered with the same woman. Determined to close this chapter, I arranged for DNA testing during the summertime. I flew to Florida to pick up both of my children and brought them back to Lawrence. Yet even before receiving the results, God was preparing my heart for the possibility that my daughter may not be biologically mine. I had always harbored doubts about my son as well, as he looked quite different from his sister. Two weeks after the test, I received the results that confirmed the boy was indeed my biological child, while the girl was not. Although I initially struggled with denial, I realized that God had been preparing me for this revelation. When I returned home, I fell to my knees, thanking the Lord for His preparation and finding solace in His presence during such a challenging time.

Motivated to continue improving myself, I made the decision to pursue education. I enrolled in a Bible Institute and worked towards earning my GED. By God's grace, I successfully completed both endeavors. This brought immense joy to my parents, who had never witnessed me receive a diploma. They proudly celebrated my achievements as I walked across the stage on June 13, 2014, for my GED, and on June 18, 2014, for the Bible Institute.

As I reflect on this journey, I hold on to the powerful words of Philippians 4:13: "I can do all things through Him who gives me strength." My unshakeable trust in God has revealed His unwavering faithfulness in my life, especially during times of weakness, where His mighty hand has consistently guided and uplifted me.

New Experiences with God

I found a job as a machine operator, finally! I have found a way to make legal money. I felt a strong sense of responsibility, knowing that I was finally doing things right. I believed that God was pleased with my decision. I became a leader of the youth at my church. There was a couple who served as youth pastors, and we became very close. Despite being 23 years old, I still considered myself part of the youth because of my past experiences growing up on the streets.had started at the age of 13.

My spiritual life was flourishing, and I felt an

incredible love for always being in God's presence. I knew that this was my identity and that my life now had purpose in this world. The day of my baptism was fast approaching, and I couldn't contain my excitement. The church services were filled with an intense energy, and God's presence was evident. I didn't fully understand it at first, but I witnessed people dancing in the spirit and speaking in tongues. Preachers would come forward with a powerful word from God, and I also witnessed people falling under God's presence and even experiencing demonic manifestations. I prayed to God, asking Him to use me if this was truly from Him. I wanted to experience the same things others were experiencing. Ever since my conversion, I had been testifying to everyone I met. I shared about the power of God and how He had shown mercy in my life, pulling me out of the streets, drugs, and the music industry. People were deeply impacted by my transformation, and they often asked me about the church I attended. I would gladly provide them with the address and service times. One day, a renowned preacher named Randy Island visited our church. As soon as he picked up the microphone and smiled, God's presence filled the room like never before. In that moment, I knew that God was calling me to preach.

Finally, the day of my baptism arrived. The night before, I could hardly sleep due to my excitement. I put on a suit that my mom had gotten for me and admired myself in the mirror. I thought to myself, "Wow, I look like a preacher now." When I arrived at church that night, all the individuals who were going to be baptized were present, along with the congregation. The atmosphere was charged with anticipation. We changed into white robes and as we prepared, the worship team began to sing. It felt as if angels were filling the church, serving as witnesses to this sacred moment. The time had come, and it was finally my turn. I stepped into the water while the pastor prayed over me. As I resurfaced, I felt an overwhelming sense of change. It was as if God was smiling down on me. Tears streamed down my face, and I could tangibly feel God's presence surrounding me. After we all finished getting baptized, the pastor's wife took the microphone and asked if any of us wanted to share our experiences. Four of us, including me, decided to testify. When I spoke and shared a little bit of my testimony, people were amazed. They couldn't imagine where God had taken me from.

Throughout my journey, I often experienced spiritual encounters where I felt unable to speak, as if someone was weighing me down. In those moments, I would rebuke it in my mind, and eventually, it would release its hold on me. My heart would race, and my breathing would become heavy. I knew that the enemy was not happy with my newfound closeness to God, considering I had served as his puppet for many years.

God would often reveal His plans to me through dreams, showing me preaching to multitudes. I witnessed people receiving liberation, healing, and much more. These dreams made me aware that God was preparing me for greater things. As my faith grew, I was asked to testify at a youth service one Friday. Although I was nervous, I wanted to be obedient to God's will. Deep inside, I prayed that God would use me according to His people's needs. The Friday arrived, and I remember my first preaching experience had a significant impact. Many individuals were moved to tears during my sermon. In the middle of it, I called a person up and shared a word of God with them, which resulted in their tears flowing freely. That night, God used me in ways I never thought possible. Many received new strength for God's glory through His powerful word.

The dreams I had about preaching became a reality faster than I could have anticipated. I started receiving invitations from various places to share my testimony.

I also witnessed how God began using me in prophecy. I encountered individuals who were possessed by demonic spirits, and through the power of the Holy Spirit, they were set free. At the end of the day, my sole desire was to win souls for Christ. I distinctly remember yearning to speak in tongues, but I had not received the gift yet. Every time a preacher made an altar call, I would fervently praise God, hoping that this would be the moment I would receive the gift. I felt a sense of sadness when it didn't happen, and I questioned if there was something wrong with me. Although God remained silent, my faith continued to grow each passing day. I firmly believed that God was with me and that He had amazing plans in store.

On one birthday, I made the decision to fast until 6 p.m. It felt like God was preparing me for something significant that evening. After finishing work, I quickly took a shower before meeting my parents at my mom's beauty salon. They had planned to take me out to eat for my birthday. Although I intended to continue the fast until we reached the restaurant, an unexpected encounter awaited me at the salon. As I greeted everyone, a Brazilian lady appeared seemingly out of nowhere. Our eyes met, but something in my spirit didn't feel right. The Holy Spirit impressed upon me that I needed to prepare myself, as I would be delivering this woman from possession. Initially, I began silently rebuking her from a distance, but God encouraged me to approach her and offer to pray for her. Miraculously, as soon as we started talking, an elder woman from my church arrived at the salon. She too felt led to be there. I invited her to join me, and together we began to pray for the young lady.

God truly works in mysterious ways, for as soon as we started praying, the woman manifested a violent reaction. Everyone presents in the salon became frightened and hurriedly left. Despite the chaos, I felt an overwhelming sense of authority and knew that God was with me. The possessed woman lunged at me aggressively, but suddenly froze and collapsed to the ground. She began screaming, admitting, "We are many demons." I commanded the legion of demons in Jesus' name to depart from her body. It took us 45 minutes of fervent prayer to set her free. As we lifted her up, her countenance had completely transformed, evidence of the power and strength of God. Overwhelmed with gratitude, she wept, and we praised God in that moment. While these experiences were undeniably blessings, they were not without their fair share of battles. Nonetheless, my relationship with God continued to grow, and He continued to use me as a vessel for His work. On one occasion, I attended a house service where many individuals were moved by my testimony and came to accept Jesus. This fueled my determination and deepened my hunger and devotion for God.

During a youth service, I was given the opportunity to preach. Prior to the service, I sought God's guidance, asking Him what He wanted me to share with His people. As I delivered the message, a lady in the congregation began manifesting strange behavior. She moved towards the altar, contorting her face in a disconcerting manner. Suddenly, she fell to the ground. After the service, she testified that when she looked up, she saw someone dressed in white standing behind me. I was astonished, realizing how God had placed His angel there for my protection. These are but a few of the remarkable testimonies I have witnessed while faithfully serving God. Another profound experience occurred when I embarked on a three-day fast, surviving solely on water, confined to the basement. The first night passed quietly, but I held onto faith, trusting that God would speak to me.

Eventually, I embarked on a trip to the Dominican Republic to preach in twelve churches. On the second day of my fast, God revealed to me that as I prayed and sought His presence, He was simultaneously breaking chains within my family. Initially, I didn't grasp the full meaning of His words, but upon completing the fast, I discovered that my sister had returned to God after backsliding. The third day of the fast proved to be different. I explicitly asked God for a hug, and around 3 a.m., I felt a fiery presence enveloping me. It was as if someone was embracing me, and I was moved to tears. In that moment, I knew without a doubt that God was with me, providing incredible comfort, and assuring me of His presence. These experiences represent just a few of the remarkable encounters I have had while faithfully serving God.

My Fall

Twice a year, our church organized youth camps where young people from all over the New England region would come together for three days of powerful worship, inspiring messages, and conferences led by different churches and preachers. These experiences allowed us to truly feel God's presence. The energy and unity felt like we were walking on clouds, and each time I left camp, I returned home renewed and on fire for God.

God opened many doors for me during this time. I

joined the prison ministry, and together with the youth pastors, we brought small services to people's homes every Wednesday. My spiritual life was flourishing, and as I continued to follow God's will, He used me in even deeper and more profound ways. Witnessing people being restored and chains being broken was a tremendous blessing. The prison ministry was particularly impactful. Every Sunday of the month, a fellow brother from my church and I would visit the prison to share our testimonies and bring God's word to the inmates. They could relate to my story, and they were filled with excitement when it was our time to fellowship with them. I saw men moved to tears, touched by the power of God. Everything we did was to glorify Jesus, and in that environment, they called me Pastor Tony. I got married and became a father to two children, Analys and Josias, adding to my family with Nathaniel, my oldest child who lived in Florida. Although outwardly it seemed like things were going well, my home life became challenging because my children's mother did not share the same vision as me. Our relationship started to crumble, and we sought counseling to salvage what remained. I tried to stand firm, but my prayer life began to waver. Amidst the difficulties, I continued to fight for my family.

I also started working with the men's society, which was different from the youth society but fitting for my season of adulthood. Additionally, I began receiving invitations to preach at various churches and eventually became an evangelist for the M.I. Pentecostal Church. It was a blessing to see my life following the right path, but the battles at home grew harder. I struggled with a lack of support from my fellow church members, feeling discouraged even though I should have kept my eyes fixed on God. Then, the COVID-19 pandemic hit, and my prayer life and pursuit of God suffered. During this time, my partner, who was no longer interested in serving God, influenced me negatively. Regrettably, I made the worst decision of my life by turning my back on God and returning to the ways of the world.

I started indulging in smoking THC vapes, drinking alcohol with higher percentages, and seeking other substances to satisfy my desires. Little by little, I found myself becoming the person I once was, falling further away from the path of righteousness that I had once walked. Please note that promoting or glorifying the use of drugs and alcohol is not appropriate. It is important to focus on the positive aspects of your story and the journey towards redemption and renewal.

Matthew 12:43-45 states, "When an impure spirit comes out of a person, it goes through arid places seeking rest and does not find it. Then it says, 'I will return to the house I left.' When it arrives, it finds the house unoccupied, swept clean and put in order. Then it goes and takes with it seven other spirits more wicked than itself, and they go in and live there. And the final condition of that person is worse than the first. That is how it will be with this wicked generation."

I found myself in a worse condition than before. Despite previously being a servant of God and having people look up to me, I had returned to my old ways. One of my weaknesses was music, so I began making music again. Additionally, I started a health challenge and successfully lost over 50lbs in less than 8 months. I was thrilled with my physical transformation and became obsessed with staying in shape. I engaged in various exercises and felt like I was in the best shape of my life. However, Christians need to be cautious and maintain a balanced approach to their health. Being overly focused on physical appearance can lead us astray from God. It may drive us to dress in a way that pleases ourselves rather than pleasing God.

Turning my back on God was both strange and shocking for my friends, as they had witnessed my complete transformation. They couldn't understand why I suddenly desired to smoke and spend time with my old companions. Life had changed so much compared to my previous life on the streets. The younger generation seemed so cold-hearted and fast-paced that I felt completely out of place. My friend, Fred, expressed his disappointment, saying, "I'm glad you're back hanging out, but I'd rather see you with a Bible in your hand." His words were a wake-up call, but my rebellious spirit prevented me from heeding them.

I began drinking more and smoking every day. Despite my physical transformation, I was hiding the pain of how I had failed God. I became more aggressive and easily angered, lacking stability. This realization hit me hard because deep inside, all I truly wanted was to serve God for the rest of my life. Now, I found myself drifting further away from Him.

Sin creates a separation between God and humanity. While I expected my brothers and sisters from church to reach out, very few did. I felt alone, empty, and lost. I started spending time with my older brother, who initially didn't want to smoke with me due to his pride in how much I had changed when I found God. Junior told me, "Brother, to be honest, I don't want to smoke with you, but since you're a grown man, let's do it."

Far from God

Being far from God doesn't even begin to describe the state of my spiritual life. It was as if everything God had shown me and how He had used me in the past was discarded. I found myself frequenting the studio, connecting with different individuals involved in the music industry. I believed that through music, drugs, and alcohol, I could erase the pain I was feeling. Little did I realize; I was merely numbing it temporarily and seeking a distraction.

As I distanced myself further from God, I could feel

the darkness consuming me. I returned to the club scene and my music began gaining traction on platforms like Spotify, Apple Music, and social media. However, this time was different because the industry was fraught with violence, and everyone knew about my Christian background of over 8 years. It left people questioning. Deep inside, despite turning my back on God, I was haunted by the truth of His calling on my life.

One night, around 3 a.m., while hanging out with my brother and his friends, he made a striking observation. He said, "It's crazy how you were once a Christian and now you've gone back. That's why I don't feel the need to go to church. It's like you were on a plane, about to land, and you jumped out." I couldn't help but feel convicted as I understood that God was speaking to me through my brother's words. I had been on the right path, in the safety of Jesus' plane, and I had chosen to jump out, taking a risk in life. That night, I left home in shock, and in my state of numbness, I rolled up some weed and started smoking.

Another night, my brother's friend began talking about God. I found it difficult to listen because I knew God was using them to reach out to me, to open my eyes to the fact that when He has a purpose with someone, He will pursue them no matter how far they try to run. But instead, I responded in anger and frustration, telling them that I was tired of hearing about God. I believed that I didn't come from this path.

In retrospect, I realized I had become the modern-day version of Jonah or the prodigal son from the Bible.

Jonah 1:1-3 states, "The word of the Lord came to Jonah son of Amittai: 'Go to the great city of Nineveh and preach against it because its wickedness has come up before me.' But Jonah ran away from the Lord and headed for Tarshish. He went down to Joppa, where he found a ship bound for that port. After paying the fare, he went aboard and sailed for Tarshish."

Luke 15:11-13 tells the story of the prodigal son. It says, "Jesus continued: 'There was a man who had two sons. The younger one said to his father, 'Father, give me my share of the estate.' So, he divided his property between them. Not long after that, the younger son got together all he had, set off for a distant country and there squandered his wealth in wild living.'"

Similarly, I had run away from God's calling, going from preaching to returning to my old ways. However, this kind of journey comes with consequences, and many individuals don't find their way back to God again.

My life became incredibly unstable, as I became lost and empty. Despite seeming content on the outside, I was broken within. Although I was in the best physical shape of my life and other things seemed to be falling into place, I never felt truly satisfied. It was as if I yearned for more and more. My anger intensified, leading me to confront and even pick fights with those who provoked me. My children became afraid as they witnessed the changes in me, feeling that I was no longer myself. I longed to have God in my heart again, but I was overcome with shame and couldn't bring myself to pray or ask for forgiveness.

As I pursued my music career, I had the opportunity to connect with influential people in the industry. One day, I drove all the way to New York to work on three projects I had lined up. It just so happened that right next door, three famous rappers whom I had admired since I was young were performing. Their names were Styles and Fame. I was thrilled to be in the same vicinity as them while I worked on my songs, and I couldn't resist asking for a picture. They graciously agreed and even commented on my dedication to my craft. After completing the music, I embarked on the long journey back to Lawrence, which took three and a half hours due to the lack of traffic. By the time I arrived home, the sun was already up, and I immediately fell into a deep sleep. It wasn't until around 2 p.m. that day that I woke up.

Focused on the Music

I was incredibly determined to forge ahead with my music career. However, there was one aspect that I couldn't bring myself to fully embrace: the culture of the streets. While the popular music of the time glorified violence and disrespect, I chose to stay true to my old-school style and focus on sharing my personal experiences. I noticed a shift as people started to listen to my music and appreciate my message and unique voice. Encouraged by this response, I decided to create two five-track demos titled "Now or Never" and "It's About That Time."

Things were progressing in my music career. The number of streams on Spotify, views on YouTube, and followers on Instagram were increasing. People started reaching out to me for collaborations, and it felt like things were going well, even though deep down I knew this wasn't where I should be. However, as time went on, I found myself becoming more involved in the aggressive street lifestyle and turning to alcohol. Running away from God left me feeling empty. Some nights, tears would fall from my face as I looked at my innocent yet confused children. They would ask me why we didn't go to church anymore, and I would tell them that I was too busy but promised we would go soon. It broke my heart to see them growing up without the church in their lives. I had lost control over my own life and desperately needed a breakthrough. I knew I was in the wrong, but I continued down the destructive path, ignoring the truth. I knew I had become an enemy of God, once his child and friend but now his adversary.

Romans 8:7 reminds us that when we are controlled by our human nature, we become enemies of God. We disobey His laws and, in fact, are incapable of obeying them. Those who follow their human nature cannot please God.

1 John 2:15-17 also reminds us not to love the world or anything in it. When we are consumed by the desires of the flesh, the allure of material possessions, and the pride of life, we are aligning ourselves with the world and not with the Father. The world and its desires will fade away, but those who do the will of God will have eternal life.

I couldn't imagine going back to church at that point. I felt like a hypocrite, and I also didn't receive any support from the church community. I don't mean to make excuses, as salvation is an individual journey, but I no longer felt the comfort and support I once had.

Then, a show opportunity came up. I sold tickets, and I had supporters. I was excited yet nervous because it had been a long time since I last performed. The event promoters created a promotional video to give people an idea of who would be performing. My brother made me a custom shirt, and I went to pick it up with a few friends. I was ready.

A Journey of Redemption

When the show started, a few other artists went up and delivered great performances. I was in my zone, just wanting to go up and give it my all like in the old days. Finally, they called me up on stage, and my supporters were there, hyping me up. It was game time. As soon as I started performing, the crowd was captivated by my unique style and the fact that I hadn't performed in a while. They loved it, and I received handshakes and compliments on my music, with people saying they loved my voice as well.

I felt like my old self again as I basked in the praise from my friends. They commended me, saying, "I knew you were good, but not that good! You really killed it up there. You know how to entertain." This only fueled my hunger to make it in the industry. At the end of the night, chaos erupted outside the club. While walking towards my car, I noticed everyone running. When I reached my car, I discovered a dent on the top of my trunk. It was an eventful night, but I didn't get to upset about it, deciding not to involve myself as the commotion seemed to have dispersed. Once I returned home, my children started speaking to me about God. It was as if God was speaking to me through their words. My daughter would ask me to tell her a Bible story, and I couldn't bring myself to tell them a story while under the influence of drugs or alcohol. I felt immense guilt before God. One day, my youngest son told me, "Dad, you know God doesn't like you drinking beers." I would respond, "Yes, you're right. I will stop soon." Even though I wanted to continue living this fake lifestyle, my children kept me grounded and reminded me of God's presence. I realized that God was preventing me from completely losing myself.

My music career flourished as I secured more features and spent countless hours in the studio. I churned out various types of music, seeking to numb the pain and drown out God's voice. However, the more I engaged in this lifestyle, the further I felt from God, leaving me without hope. God, in His incredible mercy and unconditional love, pursued me relentlessly, no matter how far I strayed or how poorly I behaved. One of the wildest experiences I had occurred on a Friday night when a friend and I decided to go to the club. We got ready, and I left to get a haircut and find an outfit for the night. Around 8 p.m., I went to my friend's house and grabbed a bottle of liquor, intending to start drinking and smoking weed before we left. We had other friends meeting us at the club as well.

Around 10 p.m., we headed out and started driving towards the club. Everything seemed fine; my friend and I laughed, listened to some old school Hip Hop, and I even showed him some of my upcoming projects. After about 25 minutes, we arrived at the club. Before entering, we took a smoke break. The line was a bit long, but our friends called us over, so we bypassed the line and joined them inside. The atmosphere was lively, and everyone appeared to be having a good time. We made our way to the bar to grab drinks and rejoined the rest of our friends. I spotted my cousin's daughter and went up to them to say hello. I asked how they were doing and assured them that I would protect them if any issues arose. They nodded in gratitude as I walked away to rejoin my friends. As the night progressed, it eventually came to an end at 2 a.m., and we prepared to leave. When we stepped outside, I heard my music playing nearby. Intrigued, I approached the person responsible and commented, "Yo, I like that music. He's nice, right?" The person replied, "Yeah, he's one of my favorites." I then revealed that I was the artist behind the music, to which they exclaimed, "Your music is crazy!" I thanked them for their support, but my friend grabbed me and urged me to leave. Confused by the sudden rush, I thanked the people once more and departed, feeling a sense of unease and readiness to confront any potential trouble. But then my friend said something that raised my suspicions. I asked him if something was wrong and suggested that we settle whatever it was. He insisted that nothing was wrong and agreed to go along. As we were driving, I noticed that he began to laugh in a strange manner and his voice seemed different. It became clear to me that he was not himself.

I called him by his street name, but he denied it and claimed not to know who I was. Instantly, I realized that he was possessed by a demonic entity. Fear surged through me as the hairs on my body stood on end. I was terrified because I knew I was not prepared for this spiritual battle. Despite my fear, I tried to reason with my friend, desperately pleading, "This is not you; don't you understand?" I pulled over and challenged him to get out of the car and fight if necessary. I didn't know what else to do. Finally, he snapped out of it and returned to his normal self, but he was confused and unaware of what had just transpired. We continued to my friend's house, both of us still shaken by the experience. When I arrived home, I couldn't stop shaking. I had just encountered and conversed with that demon. It mocked me, knowing that I was far from God and not serving Him. This was just one of the many experiences that showed me that this spiritual battle was not a game. It was a clear warning from God urging me to turn back to Him.

Restored by God

As time went on, more and more people started listening to my music. I would often go to clubs wearing designer clothes I had custom-made for my brand, and my videos on YouTube were gaining traction. My streams continued to increase, and I even received messages from big artists on Instagram, expressing interest in working with me. However, I turned down their offers, as I wanted to remain independent. They told me to reach out anytime, as they had heard a song of mine and loved it.

While I was making strides in my music career, I held firm in my beliefs about the industry. Many may not believe it, but I was aware that many favorite rappers, entertainers, and even movie stars had made deals with the devil and participated in rituals and sacrifices. I did not want to be a part of it. I knew deep down that I wanted to return to God, even though I couldn't find the way back.

As the days passed, I found myself smoking more and more. There were moments when I was tempted to return to selling drugs, but the love I had for my children prevented me from doing so. They were everything to me. However, I felt guilty because I had previously set a great example for them when I was involved in church, but now I wasn't. They would occasionally ask me about church and when I would preach again, and I didn't have a satisfactory answer for them.

A difficult situation occurred that significantly impacted my relationship. Infidelity had occurred in the past, and I was deeply hurt by it. I tried my best to make things work, but I soon realized that it takes two people to salvage a relationship. Turning my back on God carried heavy consequences, and eventually, divorce became inevitable. Separation wasn't what I wanted, as she made the decision to leave and never return. Seeing my kids suffer and cry during this time was heart-wrenching because as adults, we can somewhat understand, but for them, it was confusing and devastating. They felt lost and left with unanswered questions. This experience made me reflect deeply on life, and I made a conscious effort to slow down and prioritize my children's mental and emotional well-being. While I continued with my music, I had to find a balance between pursuing my career and being a full-time dad. She remained minimally involved in their lives, and as a result, they were deeply hurt. I am incredibly grateful to my parents for their support and help during this challenging period.

I started receiving invitations to shows, and my music was gaining popularity in different states. I had big plans to work even harder and potentially make enough money from music to provide a better life for my kids. However, God always finds a way to pull you back in. I was getting used to being alone with my kids and always finding things to do with them, but there was still a void that couldn't be filled, especially since their mother wasn't around much. There was a show coming up where a friend of mine, who had produced three beats for me, was also performing. I felt some tension between us because he was closer to my older brother and associated with my brother's gang-affiliated friends. We all planned to go to the show together, and I invited my friend, who had a reputation for being dangerous. He arrived late, so I told him to call me when he was ready, and I would pick him up. Meanwhile, all my brother's friends, who were part of the gang, were getting to the show. I encountered my friend's cousin, the one who made the beats for me, and we had a heated confrontation. Afterward, he went inside. I pulled his cousin aside and expressed my feelings about his cousin's behavior. He tried to calm me down, acknowledging that his cousin had changed, but I had to relax. I was still upset, but I let go of the anger and went to pick up my friend. However, when I arrived, they mistakenly thought I had come for trouble, even though that wasn't my intention. My older brother criticized my actions, and while I knew he was wrong, I had to deal with it. That night, I told my close friend, "I am done with this." I felt like everyone around me was being fake, and I decided to focus on myself.

The desire to return to God grew within me. I knew I needed to do what was right, especially for the sake of my kids who were witnessing my worsening anger issues. Life had hit me hard, and I found myself facing the consequences alone with my kids. I made the decision to start attending church again, and I began visiting the house of my spiritual parents, who had become pastors. It felt good to be back, even though I may not have shown it. Everyone from the church was overjoyed to see me, as they had been praying fervently for God to open my eyes. I was grateful for those spiritual warriors who fought battles on my behalf during my weaker moments. Even though I started to visit, it took time and a humbling of myself before the Lord to fully surrender and commit to the path of righteousness.

Job 22:23 reminds us that if we return to the Almighty, we will be restored and if we remove unrighteousness from our lives, our tents will be cleansed.

In Nehemiah 1:9, God promises that if we return to Him, keep His commandments, and obey Him, He will gather us and bring us to a place where His name dwells, no matter how far away we may have strayed.

Zechariah 1:3 declares the Lord's words, urging us to return to Him so that He may also return to us, highlighting the importance of our repentance and relationship with Him.

Jeremiah 4:1 speaks of God's invitation to Israel to return to Him, putting away detestable things and remaining steadfast in their faith.

I knew that I had to return to the Lord, for my calling in Him was greater. His love is unfathomable, and Jesus willingly went to the cross knowing that we would stumble and fall. He endured the process because we all fall short of His glory. Jesus came to redeem us from our sins, granting us access to the Father in heaven.

Romans 3:23-24 reminds us that all have sinned and

fall short of God's glorious standard, but through His grace, He makes us right in His sight. This was accomplished through the sacrifice of Christ Jesus, who freed us from the penalty of our sins.

Galatians 3:13 further emphasizes that Christ redeemed us from the curse of the law by becoming a curse for us, taking our place on the cross.

Hebrews 9:15 explains that Christ is the mediator of a new covenant, offering eternal inheritance to those who are called. He died as a ransom to set us free from the sins committed under the first covenant.

These passages reassured me of God's incredible love and His desire for us to return to Him. I knew that my path forward was to surrender myself once again, repent of my sins, and embrace the redemption and freedom found only in Jesus Christ.

Acts 3:19 reminds us to repent and turn to God so that our sins may be wiped out, and we may experience times of refreshing from the Lord.

One day, God used my children to open my eyes and bring conviction to my heart. My son Josias told me, "Dad, you know God doesn't like the music I hear," and my daughter asked me one night, "Dad, can you tell me a Bible story?" It was as if God was speaking directly to me through their innocent words. Despite my own sinful habits of smoking and drinking, I realized that I needed to teach my children about God's word and His love.

A Journey of Redemption

This realization led me to take a step towards returning to God. I never expected His love to be so great that even though I had drifted away, He was still willing to receive me with open arms. The time had come for me to humble myself at the feet of Jesus. That night, I dressed in the same suit I used to preach in, and as I attended the church service, I eagerly awaited the altar call. When it finally came, I raised my hands and walked to the front to surrender myself to Jesus once again. Tears streamed down my face as the pastor prayed for me.

In that moment, I felt the presence of God surrounding me once again. My children were overjoyed that I had returned to God, and together, we embarked on a new journey of faith and restoration.

Men It felt so good to be back to church, I was so blinded, but God was waiting for me to come raise me up. No matter the sins you have committed may feel God will never forgive you but God it's always willing to forgive you. Just know one thing are you willing to forgive yourself. Yes, people will talk bad about you or won't believe on you converting after you fall. But God don't judge like men do. He died for you and me. So not matter the situation you're in, nor the sin you have committed God will lift you up. He will restore your testimony, and it will take time to raise but it's possible.

If you want to this prayer with me especially you don't have Christ in your heart nor never accept him to come in repeat after me. Heavenly Father, at this moment

I come before you to give you the Glory and Honor. At this time, I ask you to forgive me of all my sins, come in my heart and transform me and make me new. Write my name in the book of life, also I confess Jesus died and resurrected the third day, I recognize he is the King of Kings and Lord of Lords.

Now I will pray for you! In the name of Jesus, I come before you are asking that whoever make this confession you may change their lives. That they may have an encounter with you and your presence like never before. Restore their lives and make the areas that are broken or in pain they feel start healing and putting back to place. For those that need strength may or just need a prayer may see your favor move with them and that their spiritual life becomes one with you Holy Spirit move in each of their lives and help them understand that you are in control of their lives. There is nothing impossible for you, and that's why we come to you. Lift up save and restore in Jesus name, and we say Amen!

Tested

Finally, I humbled myself before God, but little did I know, it was just the beginning. As I started attending church, I carried with me a broken spirit and overwhelming anger for allowing myself to fall into such a dark place. I often pondered the what ifs, wondering what my life would have been like had I never strayed from God's presence. Yet, during my pain, I found solace in shedding tears of repentance in God's comforting embrace. It was in those moments that I knew I was where I belonged.

Witnessing my children's tears during the separation was heart-wrenching. I knew they couldn't fully comprehend the situation. Despite the immense difficulties, I remained determined to be a pillar of support for my children. They unknowingly became my source of strength, alongside God.

I began attending different churches, seeking guidance and solace. It was not easy to come to terms with the division within my own household. Yet, I held onto my faith in God and trusted that He had a plan, even though starting anew seemed impossible.

This time, rediscovering my connection with Christ was different. I had grown older and gained more maturity. I had endured my fair share of trials, which proved instrumental in deepening my relationship with God. I am eternally grateful to all those who supported me, whether directly or indirectly, during this process of healing. Divorce is not a path I would recommend, but there are instances where it becomes inevitable. The topic of divorce often stirs mixed emotions within the church community. Some individuals, empathetic to my situation, reassured me that it was acceptable to seek separation. However, there were others who adhered to the belief that marriage should last forever. It saddened me to witness how, at times, we selectively apply biblical teachings to certain aspects of life or pass judgment without truly understanding the struggles others face. Only God has the right to judge; our role is to uplift and support those who are spiritually wounded. Whether through active assistance or fervent prayers, we must strive to lift each other up. Even though I had returned to the church, I occasionally battled confusion and guilt, feeling like a hypocrite for having backslid. Forgiving myself proved to be an arduous journey, and at one point, my testimony lay shattered on the ground. I intensified my prayers and surrendered myself to God's guidance, but the path to redemption was undeniably challenging.

To all the religious individuals who encounter those who have stumbled and struggle with recurring bad habits, it's essential to understand that they are disappointing God, not mere mortals. I do not attempt to justify or condone free-spirited sinning, but rather emphasize the importance of restoration within the community. It is regrettable that those who often judge or criticize others are frequently guilty of similar or even worse transgressions. Some may witness their own children's tribulations, which serve as a reminder that no one should point fingers at another soul. Instead, we ought to extend a helping hand and foster an environment of compassion and understanding.

1 John 2:1 says, "My little children, I am writing

these things to you so that you may not sin. But if anyone does sin, we have an advocate with the Father—Jesus Christ the righteous one."

My life has reached various milestones, and I am eternally grateful to God for always being there at the right time.

My children started participating in the kids' service at church, singing for the Lord. It brought tears to my eyes to witness them singing joyfully, finding solace in the house of God. Yet, there were also moments of sadness, as they noticed other kids with their mothers beside them while their own mother was absent. But God helped me and granted me wisdom to guide them through those difficult moments. As I continued my journey of recovery, I began reading a book by Juan Carlos Harrigan that focused on the power of prayer. I wholeheartedly recommend this book to anyone seeking to deepen their prayer life. Initially, I would spend around 15 minutes in prayer, but as my connection with God grew stronger, I found myself spending more and more time in His presence. I even began waking up at 4 a.m. to seek God's face, and I could feel myself growing spiritually.

When the New Year arrived, our church initiated a 21-day congregational fast. This period of fasting allowed me to release my burdens and surrender them into God's loving hands. It was during this time that I became acutely aware of my anger issues. One incident served as a wake-up call. While driving with my kids, a taxi ran a red light and nearly collided with us. Fuming with rage, I followed the taxi until it dropped off a passenger. I positioned my car in front of the taxi, got out, and unleashed my anger upon the driver. He cowered in fear, unable to meet my gaze. However, during my tirade, I heard a small voice - it was my daughter, calling out to me in fear. She pleaded, "Daddy, daddy, please stop."

It was in that moment of realization, as my daughter's voice cut through my fury, that I calmed down and felt an overwhelming sense of guilt. I was deeply remorseful for losing control in front of my children. What struck me even more was when my tearful daughter, still frightened, told me, "Dad, I would like to help you and pray to God to take away your anger." It was a profound revelation for me. I knew I needed to let go and surrender it all to God. If it hadn't been for that situation, I may never have recognized the depth of my anger issue. Truly, God works in mysterious ways.

My faith was being tested as I continued my journey. It was challenging, especially when confronted with circumstances that demanded I let go. I am grateful to God for revealing my flaws and guiding me towards the right path. With my life centered on raising my children, I decided to enroll them in music school. My son took up the drums, while my daughter learned to play the piano. Their enthusiasm helped fill the void in their hearts. I started relinquishing control to God, as painful as it was, knowing it was the right thing to do.

I did everything I could for my children. My eldest son came to live with me for a year, and this was the first time I had all three kids under one roof. It brought me tremendous joy to see things falling into place. My oldest and youngest sons expressed an interest in playing football, so I enrolled them in a local league. They were thrilled to be a part of it. During their first practice, the coach noticed me providing guidance to my children and asked if I would be interested in serving as an assistant coach. Without hesitation, I accepted the role. I had never been as present in my oldest son's life before, since he lived in Florida. This was my first opportunity to be more involved, and it brought me immense joy. I made it a priority to not let them down. My daughter eagerly joined us, excited to watch her brothers play.

During this journey, I had a profound experience, but I couldn't help but notice that it was consuming most of my time. As a result, my prayer life started to suffer once again. Being a single father was no easy task and the feelings of loneliness began to weigh heavily on me. Seeking guidance, I turned to my pastor who emphasized the importance of finding balance and maintaining focus. However, I found myself slowly opening doors that led me down a path of sin and away from God's pleasure. It wasn't as though I was engaging in wild parties or engaging in promiscuous behavior, but I would meet friends and flirt with them. I even started chatting with Christian girls online, initially with good intentions, but it always ended up going in the wrong direction. Deep inside, my ultimate desire was to please God.

My life became increasingly unstable. Despite the turmoil, there was a part of me that fought to reach out and ask God for help. I urge you, if you find yourself in similar situations, close these doors quickly, for they will lead to separation from God and spiritual death. God calls us to live by the Spirit, not to succumb to our fleshly desires. I found myself in various predicaments, often crying out to the Lord for a way out. And faithfully, God always lifted me up.

Sadly, many people have the tendency to approach God only when they are in need, and once their problems are solved, they walk away. But God calls us to remain steadfast during the trials.

Matthew 16:24 states, "Then Jesus said to his disciples, 'Whoever wants to be my disciple must deny themselves and take up their cross and follow me.' " It is the act of denying our fleshly desires that can be challenging.

Galatians 5:16 advises, "So I say, walk by the Spirit, and you will not gratify the desires of the flesh."

A Journey of Redemption

Romans 12:2 reminds us, "Do not conform to the pattern of this world but be transformed by the renewing of your mind. Then you will be able to test and approve what God's will is—his good, pleasing and perfect will."

God has called us to live differently, to live for Him. This world is temporary, and sometimes we find ourselves falling into the same traps. It is better to let go and take control, refusing to be influenced by the ways of the world. There is a reality beyond what our eyes can see.

2 Corinthians 4:18 encourages us, "So we fix our eyes not on what is seen, but on what is unseen, since what is seen is temporary, but what is unseen is eternal."

Matthew 6:33 teaches us, "But seek first his kingdom and his righteousness, and all these things will be given to you as well." May we continually strive to seek God's kingdom and righteousness, knowing that as we do, all other things will fall into place. Navigating through open doors can sometimes lead to unfavorable outcomes, and oftentimes, picking oneself up after a fall is no easy feat. My most significant advice to you is to stand firm and remain steadfast in God's fiery presence.

Living as a Christian may appear effortless from the outside, but in all honesty, it is far from easy. We find ourselves engaged in an internal battle with our own desires, our toughest challenge second only to contending with Satan and the spiritual forces roaming our temporary world. My goal is to ensure that when the day of redemption arrives, I make it to heaven without living a life of pretense, but rather with authenticity. It is during the most intimate moments that I strive to remain faithful to God. I understand many men are facing numerous struggles, be it addiction to drugs, women, alcohol, and so on. Some are entangled in the grip of pornography or unfaithfulness towards their spouses. However, what is the value of losing our salvation to these fleeting temptations in a transitory life that offers no guarantees? It simply doesn't add up.

God Turn all my mistakes around.

So many mistakes have plagued my life. Even though I found my way back to the Lord, it felt like an endless cycle of setbacks. I would start seeking God fervently, only to get sidetracked again. It seemed like I was going nowhere, and I felt completely alone, with no one who could truly understand me. Regrettably, I opened too many doors when I returned to the world.

Now, I can clearly see how much this has affected my walk with God. Sometimes, the enemy would implant thoughts in my head, making me believe that I am unworthy or not good enough. I found myself engulfed in battles that I had no idea how to handle. These things used to have little impact on me, but now they pose a much greater challenge. One day, I would experience a complete transformation through the power of God, but the next day, I would find myself engaging in activities that did not please Him.

For those who stand firm in their faith, I implore you to remain vigilant, as the enemy is always waiting to strike you down. Never judge others, for you never know when you too may fall and need a helping hand. To those who are still strong in the Lord, extend your kindness and support to those who are weak. Stay humble, especially when God is using you as a vessel. Many people forget that it is God who has chosen us, not the other way around.

Now, for those who are grappling with struggles and facing relentless battles, I urge you to keep fighting and endure the storms, for God will grant you victory. If you feel weak, seek spiritual assistance from fellow members of your church. If you do not have a church, seek one that can guide you along the right path.

I never thought I would find myself in the dire state I was in. When I first came to Christ, I believed that I would never return to the ways of the world. However, I found myself aimlessly wandering, unsure of where I would ultimately end up. There were times when I had a deep, unsettling feeling that something was bound to happen to me, echoing within the depths of my soul.

Thank God for His immeasurable mercy and grace. Even though I did not deserve forgiveness for my sins, Jesus chose to lay His life down on that cross

My life was relatively smooth sailing, but I yearned for a wife and someone who would truly be authentic with me. I longed for a family. Then, during a special worship service, I noticed a beautiful woman, worshipping alongside her daughters. As our eyes locked, I sensed deep within me that she was meant to be mine. However, it dawned on me that I didn't know her closely, though I had seen her before.

I took a leap of faith and reached out to her, and we began a friendship. We discovered numerous common interests, leading us to arrange a dinner together. That night, we went bowling and then shared a meal at a restaurant. We had an incredible time, filled with laughter and deep conversations about our life goals. Above all, we both shared a love for God, and all we desired was to live a life that pleased Him.

Eventually, I introduced her to my parents, and from the start, they adored her. As months went by, our feelings for each other grew stronger and deeper.

Our children were growing closer, and my kids adored my girlfriend Heidy, while her children accepted me as well. We began to forge a strong bond with each other. We knew that things didn't start off perfectly, but we were determined to make it right. Following the guidance of our pastors, we attended pre-marriage counseling, meeting once a week and studying a book together. After eight weeks of counseling, our pastor advised us that we were ready for marriage. He expressed his happiness for us, and it filled our hearts with joy. One day, I finally gathered the courage to ask the question that had been on my mind: "Will you marry me?"

She said yes!

Our family and friends helped me with the surprise. She had no idea it was coming, so the look of shock on her face was priceless. Heidy has been an incredible blessing in my life. She came into my life at a critical point in my spiritual journey. I truly believe that this was God's mysterious work.

The day of our wedding finally arrived, and we were surrounded by our loved ones. We were overflowing with happiness during the wedding ceremony. Everything went smoothly, from the delicious food to the beautiful decorations. I understand that perfection is not the goal, but I know in my heart that I have found the right woman to stand by my side. She is a prayer warrior and constantly seeks God's guidance.

Our new journey together has begun, and I kindly ask for your prayers so that we may become a source of blessing to the world and reach out to those in need God's word.

A Journey of Redemption

A Journey of Redemption

Reflection

The consequences of falling than coming back to Christ"
is a profound concept that digs deep into the human
condition and the road towards spiritual rebirth. In these
6 points, we will talk about the transformative power of
faith, also the consequences that falling away from
Christ can have on our lives, and the redemption that
occurs when we find our way back to Him.

A Journey of Redemption

The Fall from Grace

- Understanding the nature of falling away from Christ:

Understanding the nature of falling away from Christ involves recognizing the process of slowly distancing ourselves from the teachings and principles of Christianity which is fasting and prayer also reading His word. It refers to a spiritual journey where your faith weakens, resulting in a decreased commitment to following Christ's example and a drift away from a relationship with God. This can occur due to many reasons such as doubts, temptations, worldly distractions, or personal hardships. However, by seeking a deeper understanding of your faith, strengthening spiritual disciplines, and seeking guidance from other believers or spiritual mentors, one can direct this challenge and find a path back to a closer relationship with Christ.

- Looking into the consequences of wander off from our spiritual path

By looking into consequences of wandering off from our spiritual path dig into the ways in which rejecting our spiritual beliefs and practices can impact our lives. Turning away from our spiritual path may lead to a sense of disconnection, confusion, and a lack of purpose. It can also result in a loss of inner peace, increased stress, and a feeling of being wrong in life. By wandering off from our spiritual path, we may find ourselves making choices that are out of alignment with our higher values, leading to feelings of dissatisfaction and come to an understanding some sense of authenticity. Additionally, when we neglect our spiritual well-being, we may experience a weakened connection with others and a lessen the capacity for compassion and empathy. Taking the time to reflect on and realign with our spiritual path can help us regain a sense of balance, rediscover our purpose, and encourage a deeper sense of fulfillment in our lives.

- The emptiness and despair that can accompany a life without Christ

The emptiness and pain that can accompany a life without Christ refers to the deep sense of void and hopelessness that individuals may experience when they lack a spiritual connection or important belief system. Without the guidance and comfort that faith in Christ can provide, people may struggle to find purpose, fulfillment, and a sense of belonging. The absence of a

A Journey of Redemption

Jesus in our lives can leave individuals feeling lost, disconnected, and without a sense of direction. The recognition of this emptiness often focus the importance of embracing spiritual faith for many individuals seeking purpose, meaning, and redemption.

Here are a few Bible verses that speak about someone that falls of grace:

1. Genesis 3:6-7 - "So when the woman saw that the tree was good for food, and that it was a delight to the eyes, and that the tree was to be desired to make one wise, she took of its fruit and ate, and she also gave some to her husband who was with her, and he ate. Then the eyes of both were opened, and they knew that they were naked. And they sewed fig leaves together and made themselves loincloths."

2. Romans 5:12 - "Therefore, just as sin came into the world through one man, and death through sin, and so death spread to all men because all sinned."

3. Romans 3:23 - "For all have sinned and fall short of the glory of God."

4. Ephesians 2:1-3 - "And you were dead in the trespasses and sins in which you once walked, following

the course of this world, following the prince of the power of the air, the spirit that is now at work in the sons of disobedience—among whom we all once lived in the passions of our flesh, carrying out the desires of the body and the mind, and were by nature children of wrath, like the rest of mankind."

5. 1 Timothy 2:14 - "And Adam was not deceived, but the woman was deceived and became a transgressor."

These verses highlight the account in Genesis where Adam and Eve disobeyed God's command, bringing sin and its consequences into the world. They also emphasize the universal nature of sin and its impact on all people.

2. The Search for Meaning

- The fundamentals of human desire for purpose and importance

The Search for Meaning is a fundamental of human quest to find purpose and importance in life. It explores the deep-rooted desire within individuals to understand their place in the world and to create a valid existence. This search involves take a good look at life's big questions such as "What is the meaning of life?" and

A Journey of Redemption

"Why am I here?" Individuals may start on a journey of self-discovery, exploring spirituality, philosophy, and personal values to find their own unique sense of purpose and achievement. The Search for Meaning is a deeply personal journey that can lead to personal growth, fulfillment, and a greater understanding of oneself and the world.

- Searching the different paths individuals take in the search of achievement.

Searching the different paths individuals take in search of achievement is a delightful road into the diverse ways people seek meaning and pleasure in their lives. Some may pursue ordinary paths, such as building a successful career or starting a family, finding achievement in the stability and accomplishments they achieve along the way. Others may choose to search alternative routes, like begin on spiritual journey, traveling the world, or dedicating themselves to creative pursuits. Everyone's road are different, as personal interests, values, and experiences influence their choices. The pursuit of achievement is a deeply personal and personal attempt, reflecting the endless possibilities of human aspirations and the beautiful difficulty of our individual journeys.

- The temporary relief and final unhappiness found outside of Christ

"The temporary relief and final unhappiness found outside of Christ" refers to the idea that seeking achievement only in worldly pleasures or chasing will only lead to temporary satisfying your flesh, which ultimately leaves a person feeling empty and unsatisfied. This point of view suggests that true and lasting achievements can only be found in a relationship with Christ, as He offers eternal joy and purpose.

Here is a few Bible verses about searching a meaning:

1. Ecclesiastes 3:11 - "He has made everything beautiful in its time. He has also set eternity in the human heart; yet no one can fathom what God has done from beginning to end."

2. Ecclesiastes 12:13 - "Now all has been heard; here is the conclusion of the matter: Fear God and keep his commandments, for this is the duty of all mankind."

3. Proverbs 3:5-6 - "Trust in the LORD with all your heart and lean not on your own understanding; in all your ways submit to him, and he will make your paths

straight."

4. Matthew 6:33 - "But seek first his kingdom and his righteousness, and all these things will be given to you as well."

5. Psalm 42:1 - "As the deer pants for streams of water, so my soul pants for you, my God."

6. Jeremiah 29:13 - "You will seek me and find me when you seek me with all your heart."

7. Isaiah 55:6 - "Seek the LORD while he may be found; call on him while he is near."

These verses show us to trust God, seek His kingdom first, and continue to seek Him with all our hearts. They also recognize the need of humanity for meaning and purpose and emphasize the importance of a relationship with God in finding true achievements and message.

3. The Consequences of a Life Without Christ

- Disorder and confusion in personal and social lives

Without Christ, you may experience disorder and confusion in their personal and social lives. The emptiness of Christ often leads to a low of moral guidance, resulting in selfishness, dishonesty, and a disregard for others. This can over work and damage relationships, causing a breakdown in trust and communication. Also, without the love and grace found in Christ, you may face hard ship to find meaning and purpose in life, leading to feelings of emptiness and unsatisfied. Being empty of Christ relieves you of His teachings on forgiveness, compassion, and selflessness, which are basic for look after a healthy and achieve relationships. Overall, a life without Christ can leave you feeling lost, disconnected, and without a solid foundation to navigate the challenges and difficulties of life.

- The acceptance of addiction, materialism, and selfishness

The consequences of a life without Christ are far away and can be seen in the generality of addiction, materialism, and selfishness. Without a Christ being the center, you may turn to worldly pleasures and substances to fill the void within yourselves.

Addiction can take be in many forms, some examples are substance abuse, gambling, or even not having a balance with technology or social media. Not having a relationship with Christ, you may seek temporary pleasure or make excuses through these addictive behaviors. Addiction often leads to self-destruction, broken relationships, and a deepening sense of emptiness.

Another reason for facing consequences without Christ in your heart is materialism. In a society that puts first wealth, possessions, and status, you may become consumed by chasing after material wealth and success. This can bring a constant need for more, leading to a never-ending cycle of unsatisfied and disappointment.

Selfishness is also common when Christ is not in your life. Without the word of Christ to guide and inspire selflessness, you may prioritize your own needs, desires, and ambitions above others. This can lead to a lack of empathy, strained relationships, and a self-centered perspective on life.

Overall, a life without Christ can result in a lack of purpose, achievements, and true joy. Without the spiritual guidance and word of God, people can fall into destructive behaviors, prioritize material possessions, and disregard the needs of others. Embracing Christ and his word you can bring about transformation, healing, and a deeper sense of purpose in life.

- The consequences of moral relativism and the loss of spiritual compass

The consequences of a life without Christ can be profound, impacting both individuals and society. One significant consequence is moral relativism, where right and wrong are determined by personal preferences rather than objective standards. Without the guiding principles of Christ's teachings, moral relativism can lead to the erosion of ethical values and the promotion of self-centered behaviors.

Without a spiritual compass, individuals may lack a sense of purpose, meaning, and fulfillment in life. They may seek satisfaction and happiness in material possessions, power, or fleeting pleasures, which can ultimately lead to emptiness and dissatisfaction. In the absence of Christ's teachings on love, compassion, and forgiveness, relationships may be strained, and empathy for others may diminish.

On a societal level, the loss of a spiritual foundation can lead to a breakdown of social cohesion and the erosion of common values. Communities may struggle to address issues such as inequality, injustice, and violence without the moral guidance provided by Christ's teachings. Without a shared moral framework, individual and collective decision-making may prioritize self-interest over the common good.

Overall, a life without Christ can result in moral relativism, a lack of purpose and fulfillment, strained relationships, and societal challenges. Embracing Christ and his teachings can provide a true spiritual scope, guiding individuals and communities towards love, compassion, and a sense of purpose that can lead to a more fulfilling and well-balance way of life.

Here are some bible verses of some consequences of a life without Christ.

1. John 3:36 - "Whoever believes in the Son has eternal life, but whoever rejects the Son will not see life, for God's wrath remains on them."

2. Romans 6:23 - "For the wages of sin is death, but the gift of God is eternal life in Christ Jesus our Lord."

3. John 14:6 - "Jesus answered, 'I am the way and the truth and the life. No one comes to the Father except through me.'"

4. Matthew 25:41 - "Then he will say to those on his left, 'Depart from me, you cursed, into the eternal fire prepared for the devil and his angels.'"

5. Ephesians 2:12 - "Remember that at that time you were separate from Christ, excluded from citizenship in Israel and foreigners to the covenants of the promise, without hope and without God in the world."

6. 2 Thessalonians 1:9 - "They will suffer the punishment of eternal destruction, away from the presence of the Lord and from the glory of his might."

7. John 8:24 - "I told you that you would die in your sins, for unless you believe that I am he you will die in your sins."

8. Romans 14:12 - "So then each of us will give an account of himself to God."

9. Hebrews 9:27 - "Just as people are destined to die once, and after that to face judgment."

10. Matthew 7:23 - "And then will I declare to them, 'I never knew you; depart from me, you workers of lawlessness.'"

4.The path to Redemption

- Validate our need for forgiveness and spiritual healing

Validate our need for forgiveness and spiritual healing is a serious point of view of our personal growth and inner peace. It involves recognizing our past mistakes, hurts, and wrongdoings, both towards ourselves and others. By facing and accepting these problems, we create a way for healing and a true transformation change. Forgiveness allows us to let go of resentment, freeing ourselves from the bad choices of the past. Through spiritual healing, we seek to align with Jesus, restore our souls and finding comfort in a deeper connection with our inner being. Overall, make realizing our need for forgiveness and spiritual healing opens us to cultivate compassion, restore our sense of well-being, and evolve into better versions of ourselves.

- Encountering Jesus grace and love in the mist of our brokenness

Encountering Jesus grace and love in the mist of our brokenness is a life changing and deeply meaningful experience. It is in these moments that we realize that no matter our flaws and struggles, we are still loved and accepted by a Jesus. Through acts of kindness, forgiveness, and redemption, we witness the incredible power of God's love and grace to heal also bring light into our lives. His love shines through the darkest of times, offering comfort, guidance, and hope. In embracing our brokenness, we open ourselves up to receiving God's compassion and finding strength in Him to overcome obstacles. This encounter brings a deep sense of peace and sets us on a road of growth, restoration, and ultimately, a deeper connection with God.

- Accepting the life-changing power of repentance and surrender

Accepting the life-changing power of repentance and surrender means realizing the ability to acknowledge mistakes, seek forgiveness, and make positive changes in our lives. It involves letting go of our ego and control, and instead trusting in the process of personal growth and surrendering to a Jesus, by embracing these qualities, we create space for healing, growth, and positive transformation in our lives.

Here are some bible verses about the path to

redemption:

1. Romans 3:23-24: "For all have sinned and fall short of the glory of God, and all are justified freely by his grace through the redemption that came by Christ Jesus."

2. Ephesians 1:7: "In him we have redemption through his blood, the forgiveness of sins, in accordance with the riches of God's grace."

3. Colossians 1:13-14: "For he has rescued us from the dominion of darkness and brought us into the kingdom of the Son he loves, in whom we have redemption, the forgiveness of sins."

4. Ephesians 2:8-9: "For it is by grace you have been saved, through faith—and this is not from yourselves, it is the gift of God—not by works, so that no one can boast."

5. Titus 2:14: "who gave himself for us to redeem us from all wickedness and to purify for himself a people that are his very own, eager to do what is good."

6. 1 Peter 1:18-19: "For you know that it was not with perishable things such as silver or gold that you

were redeemed from the empty way of life handed down to you from your ancestors, but with the precious blood of Christ, a lamb without blemish or defect."

7. Psalm 130:7-8: "Israel, put your hope in the LORD, for with the LORD is unfailing love and with him is full redemption. He himself will redeem Israel from all their sins."

8. Isaiah 44:22: "I have swept away your offenses like a cloud, your sins like the morning mist. Return to me, for I have redeemed you."

9. Revelation 5:9: "And they sang a new song, saying: 'You are worthy to take the scroll and to open its seals, because you were slain, and with your blood you purchased for God persons from every tribe and language and people and nation.'"

10. Isaiah 55:7: "Let the wicked forsake their ways and the unrighteous their thoughts. Let them turn to the LORD, and he will have mercy on them, and to our God, for he will freely pardon."

5.The Road Back to Christ

- 6 Steps towards spiritual renewal and restoration

1. Self-reflection: Take time to self-examination and assess your current spiritual life. Reflect on your values, beliefs, and areas of life that need improvement.

2. Setting purpose: Define your purpose and goals for your spiritual path. Establish clear intentions to guide you in your path towards renewal.

3. Gratitude practice: Cultivate an attitude of gratitude by recognizing and appreciating the blessings and God has given you. This practice strengthens the connection to your inner self and helps to keep focus and let the Holy Spirit take control.

4. Engaging in spiritual practices: Explore different church activities that resonate with you, such as prayer, vigil, or reading the word of God. Go back to your first love and try to stay on the fire of God..

5. Seek spiritual guidance and support: Consider seeking spiritual guidance from spiritual leaders from your church, mentors. Surround yourself with Christian that are in the fire with God and that encourage you to be better also who can support and encourage your spiritual growth.

6. Letting go of negative vibes: letting go any negative emotions, hate, or any old things that hinder your spiritual life. Forgiveness, acceptance, and detachment can help healing and restoration.

- Overcoming shame, guilt, and doubt on our return to Christ

Overcoming shame, guilt, and doubt on our return to Christ is a process within yourself, forgiveness, and take in the love and grace of Christ. It involves realizing our past mistakes and the negative emotions they may have caused, but also understanding that Christ offers redemption and a fresh start. By realizing and accepting our shame, guilt, and doubt, we can actively seek God's forgiveness, release these burdens, and replace them with the faith, hope, and a renewed sense of purpose through Jesus. It's essential to remember that everyone experiences these emotions at some point of there lives, and by turning to Christ, we can find the strength and guidance needed to overcome them and fully include a life of spiritual growth and fulfillment.

- Finding hope, purpose, and peace in a restored relationship with Jesus

A Journey of Redemption

Finding hope, purpose, and peace in a restored relationship with Jesus refers to the road of reconnecting with one's faith and spirituality. It involves seeking guidance, and strength from a God, leading to a renewed sense of hope, finding your purpose in life, and experiencing true peace with in. This process often includes prayer, self-reflection, studying the bible, attending church services, and taking in the teachings of Jesus. Restoring a relationship with Christ can bring comfort.

Here are a few Bible verses that speak about the road back to Christ:

1. Luke 15:20 - "And he arose and came to his father. But while he was still a long way off, his father saw him and felt compassion, and ran and embraced him and kissed him." This verse comes from the parable of the prodigal son and highlights the unconditional love and forgiveness that God offers to those who turn back to Him.

2. James 4:8 - "Draw near to God, and he will draw near to you." This verse encourages us to take the first step in returning to Christ by drawing near to Him. It reminds us that as we seek Him, He will actively seek us as well.

3. 1 John 1:9 - "If we confess our sins, he is faithful and just to forgive us our sins and to cleanse us from all unrighteousness." This verse reminds us that repentance and confession of our sins is essential in the journey back to Christ. God's faithfulness and justice allow us to receive His forgiveness and be restored to a right relationship with Him.

4. Matthew 11:28-30 - "Come to me, all who labor and are heavy laden, and I will give you rest. Take my yoke upon you, and learn from me, for I am gentle and lowly in heart, and you will find rest for your souls. For my yoke is easy, and my burden is light." This verse invites those who are burdened by their sins or life's challenges to come to Jesus. It assures us that He will provide rest and guidance in our journey back to Him.

5. Psalm 51:10 - "Create in me a clean heart, O God, and renew a right spirit within me." This verse reflects the heartfelt prayer of a person seeking restoration with God. It emphasizes the need for inner transformation and renewal as we return to Christ.

Remember, these verses provide guidance and encouragement, but it is important to study the entire Bible and seek God's wisdom and understanding in your personal journey back to Him.

6. The Consequences of Returning to Christ

- Living a life by faith, love, and compassion

Living a life by faith, love, and compassion means that your actions and decisions are connected by their beliefs, values, and empathy towards others. It involves having a strong belief in Christ, that serves as a foundation for their thoughts and actions.

Faith in Christ plays a big role in shaping your life, providing hope, purpose, and guidance. It can involve trust in a God, Jesus teachings.

Living a life by faith, love, and compassion means stand up for personal growth and becoming a blessing to others. It involves making choices that align with God's purpose with you and seeking opportunities to bring light, joy, and support to those around you.

- The freedom found in surrendering to God's will

The freedom found in surrendering to God's will is the understand that there is a God guiding and directing our lives. It part of letting go of our own desires, plans, and expectations, and instead trusting in God's perfect plan and wisdom. In surrendering, we find liberation from the burden of trying to control outcomes and can experience a profound sense of peace, purpose, and fulfillment. It is the realization that God's will is in our best interest, and embracing it allows us to live with a newfound freedom, authenticity, and joy.

- The transformative power of grace and the abundant life in Christ

The life-changing power of grace refers to the incredible ability of grace, a needless divine favor, to bring about positive and significant changes in your lives. It is through grace that individuals can experience forgiveness, redemption, and a renewed sense of purpose.

The abundant life in Christ is a concept derived from the teachings of Jesus. It refers to a life that is characterized by spiritual fulfillment, joy, and a deep connection with God. This abundant life includes experiencing the fullness of God's love and grace, having a sense of peace and contentment, and living in harmony with others.

Together, the transformative power of grace and the

abundant life in Christ highlight the incredible potential for personal growth, spiritual renewal, and a truly fulfilling existence that can be found through a relationship with Jesus. It emphasizes that through grace, individuals can find healing, restoration, and a renewed purpose in life, ultimately leading to a life of abundance and fulfillment.

Here are some Bible verses about the consequences of returning to Christ:

1. 2 Chronicles 7:14: "If my people who are called by my name humble themselves and pray and seek my face and turn from their wicked ways, then I will hear from heaven and will forgive their sin and heal their land."

2. Jeremiah 15:19: "Therefore thus says the Lord: 'If you return, I will restore you, and you shall stand before me. If you utter what is precious, and not what is worthless, you shall be as my mouth. They shall turn to you, but you shall not turn to them.'"

3. Ezekiel 18:21-23: "But if a wicked person turns away from all his sins that he has committed and keeps all my statutes and does what is just and right, he shall surely live; he shall not die. None of the transgressions

that he has committed shall be remembered against him; for the righteousness that he has done he shall live. Have I any pleasure in the death of the wicked, declares the Lord God, and not rather that he should turn from his way and live?"

4. Acts 3:19: "Repent therefore, and turn back, that your sins may be blotted out,"

5. James 4:8-10: "Draw near to God, and he will draw near to you. Cleanse your hands, you sinners, and purify your hearts, you double-minded. Be wretched and mourn and weep. Let your laughter be turned to mourning and your joy to gloom. Humble yourselves before the Lord, and he will exalt you."

These verses highlight the importance of humility, repentance, and turning away from sinful ways. They also promise forgiveness, restoration, and a close relationship with God for those who choose to return to Him.

Conclusion:
In this 10-page book, we have explored the consequences of falling away than coming back to Christ. We have examined the deep yearning for purpose and fulfillment that drives us to search for meaning in

various avenues, only to find temporary satisfaction and ultimate emptiness. However, the journey back to Christ brings about redemption, restoration, and a life filled with divine purpose. May this book inspire and encourage those who have fallen away to return to the loving embrace of Christ, experiencing true freedom, joy, and the abundant life that only He can offer.